In My Own Words...

 THE BASICS

Full name   _____

Date of birth   _____

Birth place   _____

# FAVORITES

Color _____

Meal _____

Food _____

Dessert _____

Season _____

Television program _____

Celebrity, actress or actor _____

Band _____

Song _____

Book _____

Play _____

Birthday party _____

Gift received _____

Gift given _____

# A BIT MORE

What is your strongest personality characteristic? _____

Is there a personality characteristic that has held you back in life? If so, how?

_____

Do you have a story about standing up against odds for something you strongly

believe? _____

_____

Do you have a fear, superstition or phobia? _____

What is your most cherished personal possession? _____

Do you have a mentor or someone who you consider having a significant

influence over your life? _____

Do you volunteer or support a charity? _____

Who was your first presidential vote? _____

Do you consider yourself a Republican, Democrat or Independent? _____

FAMILY

 MOTHER & FATHER

What is your mother's name and heritage? _____

What is your father's name and heritage? _____

How was your family financially supported?_____

What was a favorite activity you did with your mother? _____

What is the fondest memory of your mother?_____

_____

What was a favorite activity you did with your father? _____

What is the fondest memory of your father?_____

_____

How would you describe your relationship with your parents?_____

_____

Do you have a story about your birth? _____

_____

Describe a special gift your mother or father made or gave to you? _____

_____

Did extended family or others ever live with you? _____

Do you know of any genetic illnesses within your family lineage?_____

_____

 SIBLINGS

Do you have any siblings? _____

What is the birth order and age difference? _____

_____

How would you describe your relationship growing up? _____

_____

What memories do you want to share regarding your siblings? _____

_____

_____

How would you describe your relationship now? _____

_____

 RELIGION

Were you raised in a religion? If so, what religion? _____

Did you regularly attend services as a child? _____

Did you have a family place of worship? _____

Do you consider yourself a spiritual person? _____

Do you have a religious home currently? _____

Do you serve in any capacity there? _____

Do you believe in God or a divine power? _____

Do you have a favorite verse, story or passage? _____

_____

# FRIENDS & PETS

What pets did you have as a child? _____

Did you have a favorite pet? _____

Who were your friends growing up? _____

_____

Do you still keep in touch with any of your childhood friends? _____

Did you have any favorite activities, games or sports that you played as a child?

_____

HOME & MEMORIES

How many homes did you live as a child? _____

Would you consider one a childhood home? If so, what was the address?

_____

Describe the home and neighborhood. _____

_____

Did you have a place where you liked to go to be alone? _____

Did you have a favorite toy or game? _____

Did you have any collections as a youth? _____

What childhood illnesses do you remember? _____

_____

What did you want to be when you grew up? _____

What is your happiest memory as a child? _____

_____

What is your saddest memory as a child? _____

_____

Do you remember a storm or drought? _____

What songs or stories did your parents share with you from your childhood?

_____

SCHOOL YEARS

❧ SCHOOLS ❧

Where did you go to grade school? _____

Did you go to a junior high or middle school? _____

Where did you go to high school? _____

How many students were in your graduating class? _____

How did you get to school? _____

Did you consider yourself a good student? _____

What kind of clothes did you wear to school? _____

What was your favorite subject? _____

What was your least favorite subject? _____

Did you have a favorite teacher? _____

What sports did you play in high school?_____

_____

What clubs did you participate in high school? _____

_____

 LIFE AS A TEEN

Who were your high school friends? _____

_____

Did you have a favorite teenage hangout? _____

Were you a wild child or rule follower? _____

Did you have any jobs as a teen? _____

What are your special formal dance memories? _____

_____

What dance trends were popular? _____

Did you do anything you regretted during your school years? _____

_____

# COLLEGE

Where did you attend college? _____

Did you have any financial assistance or scholarship?_____

What degree did you earn?_____

What year did you graduate? _____ Honors or awards? _____

Who were your close friends during college? _____

_____

Were you a member of a sorority or fraternity? _____

Did you participate in any organizations? _____

_____

Did you have any leadership roles? _____

Do you have any stories you would like to share? _____

_____

_____

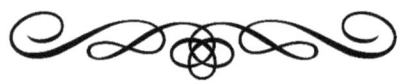

YOUNG ADULT

 DATING

Do you remember your first date? _____

_____

Do you remember your first kiss? _____

Who was your first crush? _____

Who was your first boyfriend or girlfriend? _____

Describe any serious relationships. _____

_____

❦ DRIVING ❦

What was your first car? _____

How old were you when you got your first car? _____

Do you remember how much it cost? _____

What driving experiences would you like to share? _____

_____

What has been your favorite car? _____

❦ MILITARY ❦

What branch of the military did you serve? _____

How many years did you serve? _____

What rank did you achieve? _____

What experiences would you like to share? _____

_____

CAREER

What was your first job after schooling?_____

What was your starting salary? _____

Do you have a memory you would like to share about your first job? _____

_____

Where did you live at the time? _____

Did you every change careers, job location or job position? _____

_____

If so, why did you change?_____

_____

What do you consider your greatest achievement in your career? _____

_____

Do you ever wish you had pursued a different career?_____

Was there a point when you told yourself "I've made it."?_____

_____

# A BIT MORE

What special vacations did you take as a young adult? _____

_____

What are your hobbies or interests ? _____

Would you say or would someone else say you have a talent? _____

_____

If you could return to your youth, is there anything you would change or do

differently? _____

_____

What would you consider a major challenge in your life? _____

What is the most significant change you see in yourself as you have matured?

_____

What morals are most important to you? _____

WEDDING BELLS

 COURTING THE BETTER HALF

How did you meet your spouse? _____

What was the first thing you noticed about him or her? _____

How old were you? _____ How long did you date before getting married? _____

What did you do on your first date? _____

_____

Do you have a story about your first kiss? _____

Describe the proposal. _____

_____

When were you married? _____ Where were you married? _____

Describe your wedding day. _____

_____

_____

Describe your reception. _____

_____

Describe your honeymoon. _____

_____

 # MARRIED YEARS

What characteristics did you love most about him or her? _____

Were there any habits he or she had that you didn't like? _____

Were there any habits you had that he/she didn't like? _____

What is the most romantic thing he or she did for you? _____

What is the most romantic thing you did for him/her?_____

Where did you live when you were first married?_____

Did you have a favorite home?_____

What was your favorite vacation you took together? _____

What was your favorite activity you did together? _____

Have there been any other marriages? _____

CHILDREN

 CHILDREN

How old were you when you had your first child? _____ Were you hoping

for a boy or girl? _____

Did you have any challenges with pregnancy?_____

How did you tell your spouse? _____

How did you share the news with parents and family?_____

How many children did you have? _____ How many years apart? _____

Do you have any delivery stories? _____

_____

Do you have a story of adoption?_____

How did you choose their names?_____

_____

What would you say is each child's strongest attribute?_____

_____

Share a fond memory of each child._____

_____

_____

Do you have any grandchildren? _____

Do you have any great grandchildren?_____

# TRADITIONS

What activities or games did you enjoy with your children? _____

_____

What type of family vacations did you take with your children? _____

_____

Do you have a favorite? _____

Do you have any holiday traditions with your family? _____

_____

_____

Do you have any favorite holiday recipes? _____

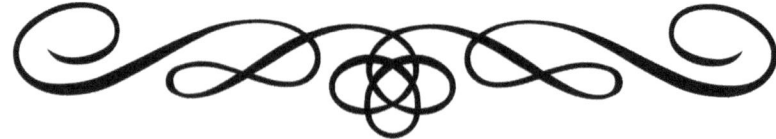

LEGACY

✤ YOUR LEGACY ✤

What accomplishment are you most proud? _____

What is the best advice you have ever given? _____

_____

What is the best advice you have ever received? _____

_____

Do you have a story of forgiveness? _____

_____

What would you consider the happiest day or period of your life? _____

_____

What is most important to you now? _____

What are you most grateful? _____

If today was your last day on earth, how would you like your friends and family

to remember you? _____

_____

_____

What is something you would like to hand down from yourself or an ancestor

that is physical, spiritual or emotional for future generations? _____

_____

What is your family legacy? _____

_____

Thoughts and memories submitted by _____

❀ A SPECIAL NOTE ❀

This heirloom memory book allows you to record and illustrate your memories spanning from childhood through marriage and children establishing a legacy for your loved ones and generations to come. The pages have large print to make recording easy. Space is provided for photos with suggestions below making it easy to gather pictures to frame in the album.

Photo Suggestions for Sections:

Basics - birth or baby (5 x 7 or 4 x 6 possible)

Favorites - birthday party, special gift (4 x 6)

A Bit More - cherished personal possession, mentor, charitable work (4 x 6)

Family Mother and Father - parents full page

Siblings - sibling (4 x 6)

Religion - service, sacrament (4 x 6)

Friends and Pets - childhood friends, pets (5 x 7 or 4 x 6 possible)

Home and Memories - childhood home - full page

School - schools, graduating class, sports, activities (3 x 5 and full page)

Life As A Teen - high school friends, dance (5 x 7 or 4 x 6 possible)

College - graduation or Greek (4 x 6 and 2 full pages)

Young Adult - (full page)

Dating - (5 x 7 or 4 x 6 possible)

Driving and Military - car or military (4 x 6)

Career - achievement, award, group (4 x 6)

A Bit More - vacation as young adult (4 x 6)

Wedding Bells - (full page)

Courting - (full page)

Married Years - (5 x 7 or 4 x 6 possible)

Married Years - vacation, home, anniversary (full page)

Children - children (full page)

Children - children's families, grandchildren, great grandchildren (full page)

Traditions - holidays (5 x 7 or 4 x 6 possible)

Traditions - holidays and family vacations (full page)

Legacy - recent photo (full page)

A Special Note - a place for a letter to your family or a note from someone special to you

Lightning Source UK Ltd.
Milton Keynes UK
UKHW05n0605070818
326831UK00003B/19/P